AF207139

Affirmations for Dads:
21 Lessons in Minding Your Fatherhood

Affirmations for Dads: 21 Lessons in Minding Your Fatherhood is a powerful tool for Fathers who recognize the importance of not only their physical strength and fortitude, but also inner-stand the significance of their mental, emotional, and spiritual power. These are 21 affirmations that will change your life!

Namaste, is translated, the light in me recognizes the light in you. These affirmations are here for you right now, at this moment. They affirm the balance already present within you. Commit to yourself for the next 21 days to care for the parts of you that your mind cannot reach. Men are culturally conditioned in this country. Begin your process of unearthing the layers of your authentic self.

Affirmations for Dads sparks your metaphysical conversation with I Am. Your ability to be true to yourself gives you the best chance to realize your purpose in this life. It is your optimal living that creates more positive life and energy in this world. This book helps fathers work smarter and not harder at fatherhood. The rhythm that jumps off the pages of this book is inspirational to all.

Affirmations *for Dads*

21 Lessons in Minding Your Fatherhood

written by
Changa Bell

Affirmations for Dads
21 Lessons in Minding Your Fatherhood

Photographed by: Changa Bell and Devonna Bell
Wedding Ring Photo by Timothy Christmas

ISBN 978-0-692-92720-5
1. Affirmations 2. Fatherhood 3. Mindfulness 4. Sprituality

Printed in the United States of America

www.changabell.com

Book design by Devonna Bell

Dedicated to Lester Murphy, Edward Bateman, Thomas H. Bell Sr., Thomas H. Bell Jr., Michael L. Bowie Sr., Michael L. Bowie, Jr. and Dads everywhere.

Special thanks to David Miller of Dare To Be King, LLC

Affirmations
for Dads

21 Lessons in Minding Your Fatherhood

written by
Changa Bell

Contents

Preface

In Affirmations for Dads, I chose African drums as my visual motif. My reasoning stems from the observation that West African drums symbolize strength, mathematics, synchronicity, high consciousness, patriarchy, and communication.

It is hard for most ethnicities to imagine no direct tie to their ancestral linage. A primary reason many African-Americans operate in familial and cultural dysfunction is our lack of true self knowledge, ancestral awareness and patriarchal insight. We are often culturally and spiritually displaced. In archetypal models of story structure every "hero" has an original story, but when your current existence appears to stem from a baseless, composite, slave-narrative, provided by cultural disrupters and conquerors, it is often a challenge not to feel orphaned by history. It is extremely difficult to re-imagine oneself as a "hero".

But the drum unites. It is a codified messaging system of communication across worlds: physical, spiritual, and emotional. Many tribal systems and people of West Africa use the drum for critical aspects of life and living, not just entertainment. Specifically, the Djembe, my dad's drum of choice, originates from a tribal meaning "Anke die, anke be" which means "everyone gather together in peace." The drum, rather than being an orphan of African born people, is a father to many countries and cultures in the "Motherland". My friend, who was born and raised on continental Africa, and who has traveled many countries around the world, once told me that in her experience, "Africans are the same everywhere; our culture is in our DNA," she said.

My dad has been a djembe drummer in Baltimore City for over 50 years. He has trained with many famous Senegalese master drummers and learned to perfect his craft. I recall him teaching me basic African rhythms as a boy of only two years old; those rhythms have been the source for both revival and survival over the course of my life. Like the ever present and pervasive sound of "OM," African rhythms pulse in the DNA of every cell of my body as I inhale and exhale. The djembe, for me, has not only served as a symbol of my biological father, but as a symbol of my ancestral fathers, which date back to the 12th Century and beyond. The djembe represents unity, strength and communication across time and borders. Furthermore, today, we find that African drums extend beyond barriers of culture, gender, race and ethnicity. The language of the drum is truly universal. It is a coded dialect that unlocks chakras and energy centers of the mind, heart and being, and leads all who follow to spiritual enlightenment. For me, there was no other visual theme for an affirmation book about Fatherhood, 'Dadhood' or 'Babahood,' other than the African drum. May the words, spirit and images of this book inspire you to live to the distinct beat and purpose of your heart.

Introduction

The drum is the sound and frequency of life. It is the syncopatic reflection of rivers and storms -- the pitter patter of rainbows and the rhythm of every heart. The drum is ancestry and it's frequencies and rhythm lay up for centuries to come. In my mind, African drums symbolize my father -- he is the reason I came to Earth. Therefore, for me, the drum is family and it is my life's song. I hope you will enjoy the rhythm of this book. May it echo within the pounding of your heart for the enjoyment of everyone!

I am he,
and he is me.

Children have never been
very good at listening to their
elders,
But they have never failed
to imitate them.
James A. Baldwin

Fatherhood 1

There is no single more important role than fatherhood. When we step forward with actions to produce a baby, then we must provide for, and protect their very being. The life of a child is like water in a canyon, without two sides the energy will spill forth, dissipate and dry out in the sun. However, with both banks to guide it, the energy and flow of the water has clear direction. And while it may have times of blockage, stillness and turmoil, the river always makes it to the larger and more vast destiny of the ocean.

Affirmation

I lift up my hands to show surrender for true love. I am a steward, a vigilant watchman, a protector, a provider, and a vessel of God.

Paternal Nurturing 2

There is no sweeter memory than that of my grandfather's and father's whiskers—that five o'clock shadow—cutting into my delicate face as a child. The smell of a cigarette or cigar, and the sticky scent of essential oils lingered on my skin. Loving, hugging and kissing your little boys doesn't make them or you 'soft' or 'weak'. It only brings memories of happiness and joy that lasts a lifetime. Say openly and often, with strength and sincerity, that you love your children. Nothing expresses love more than when your face and eyes light up when your children enter the room. While they are still little, if they run out to greet you when you get home from work, run toward them and greet them back with equal fervor. There is no stronger man, nor more nurturing man, than the one that expresses love in both action and word.

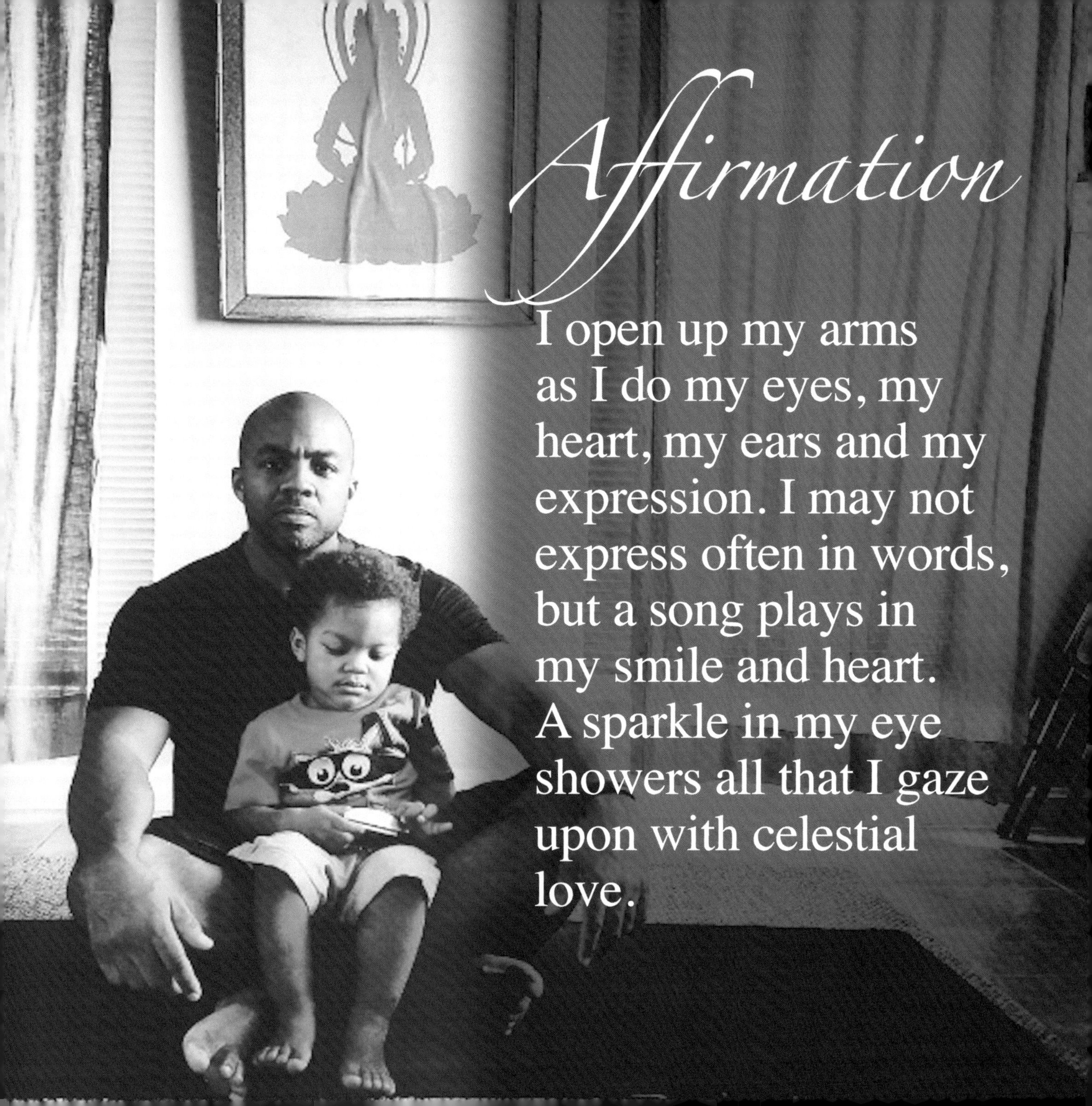

Affirmation
I open up my arms
as I do my eyes, my
heart, my ears and my
expression. I may not
express often in words,
but a song plays in
my smile and heart.
A sparkle in my eye
showers all that I gaze
upon with celestial
love.

Love & Romance 3

Neither the love or the romance created the child. Nor was it the biological process of sperm and ovum. It was the cosmic spark; it is pure evidence of the Light of the Creator existing in you. Remember this always, and unconditional love will flow from you. When this experience is in your heart, each smile, each look and every breath you breathe quietly in her ear will be romantic.

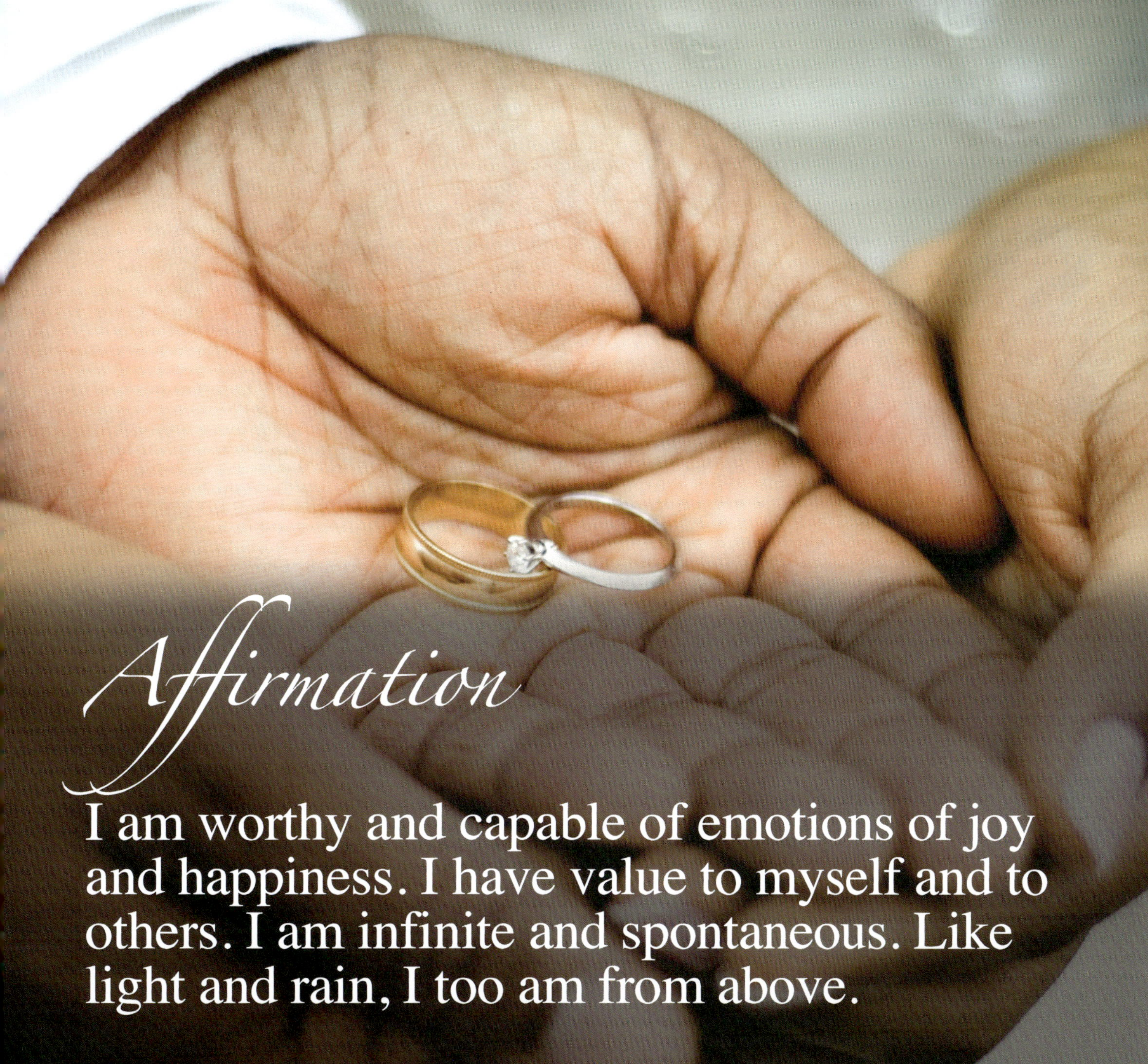

Affirmation

I am worthy and capable of emotions of joy and happiness. I have value to myself and to others. I am infinite and spontaneous. Like light and rain, I too am from above.

Education & Intellect 4

The yoga sutras state, that all pain and suffering is brought on by ignorance; therefore, seek higher knowledge to lessen the impact of trivial passions in life. There will always be death, sorrow and loss, but those are temporal. Insight leads to oversight and oversight leads to out-of-sight (faith, belief, trust, and wisdom). All paths of enlightenment begin with education. Always be a student of life and life will share revelation with you.

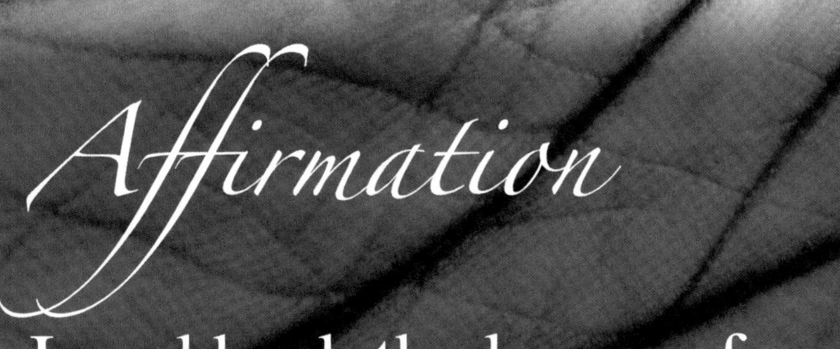

Affirmation

I peel back the layers of social, emotional, economic and physical conditioning to recognize that the one true source of all learning is me. When I learn myself, I am wise to all.

Maturity 5

Over 40 or gray hair doesn't make you mature. Length of time at a job or in a religious institution doesn't make you mature. Home and car ownership, good credit and parenthood does not make you mature. Nor does a non-sensical, stoic attitude. Maturity comes from spiritual growth, progress on a metaphysical plane. No man has a monopoly on health. Remain open to your individualized life experience; it is crafted and customized for you by you. This is maturity.

Affirmation

I am stitched from the fabric of the
Universe. I evolve and grow with time. From
experience to wisdom, I am alive with time.

Coming Home After A Hard Day at Work 6

It is too cliché and ineffective to say "leave all your problems at the door". Your snapshot of being all depends on where you are in this particular moment of your spiritual journey. If you are operating in your purpose, you will want to share your day with your loved ones. If you are not, you will not, or perhaps may want to use greater discretion when sharing. There is no need to bring negative energy into your home and better yet the mind/body. Instead, develop a ritual or discipline to quickly get rid of unwanted energy. In short, no day at work is "hard, per se," rather, it is your interpretation of your experience as you work, which forms your reality. Professional football players, arctic fishermen, and urban firemen, all have challenging work, yet they revel in the difficulty of the work because their chosen craft is designed exclusively for them. The challenge and the resulting accomplishment is part of their DNA. If work is "hard," leave your work. You may not be on your path.

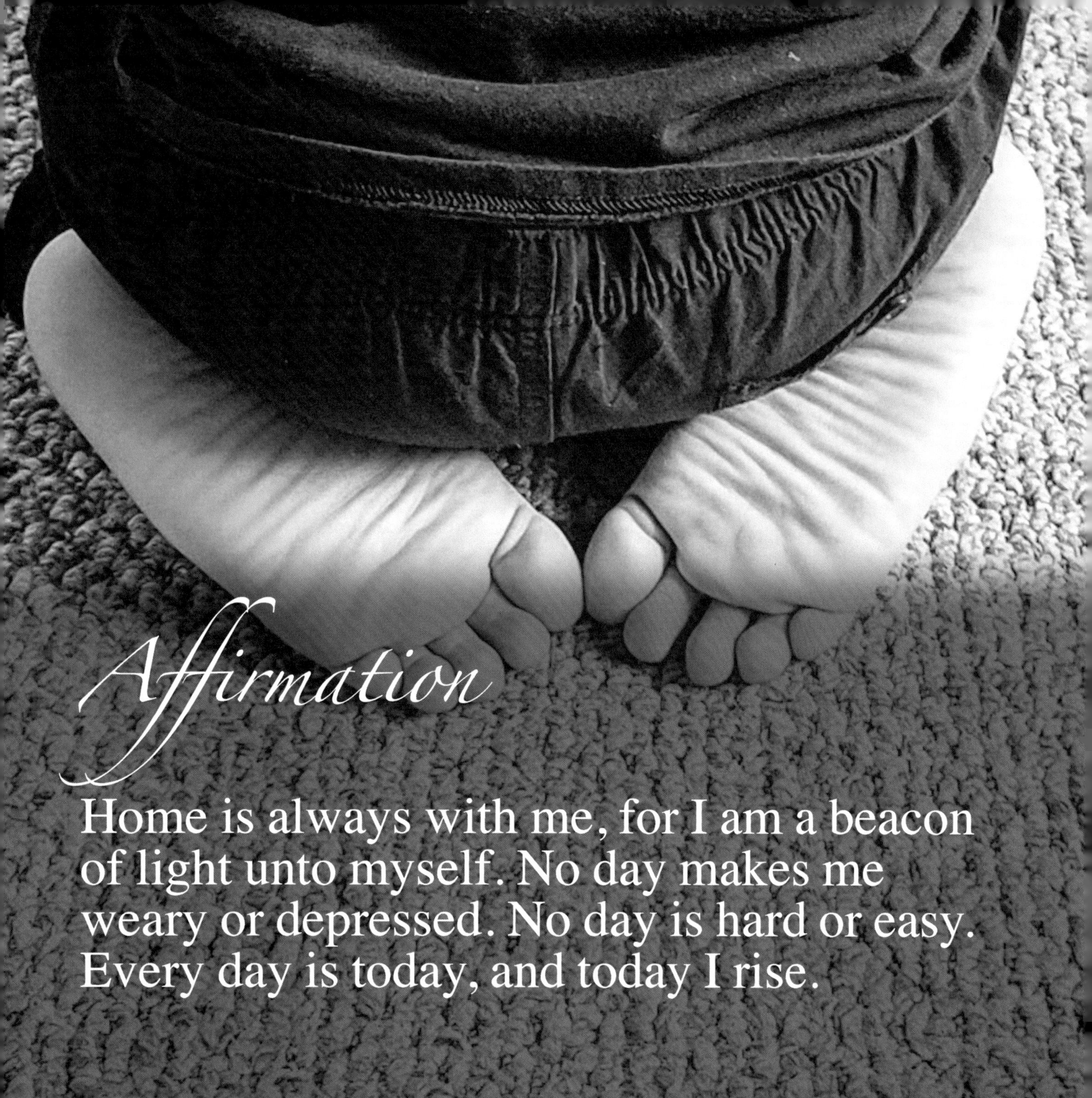

Affirmation

Home is always with me, for I am a beacon
of light unto myself. No day makes me
weary or depressed. No day is hard or easy.
Every day is today, and today I rise.

Vulnerability 7

Vulnerability takes patience; it is a craft. Work little by little to artfully master revelation of vulnerability in your life. Open and close your heart and emotions methodically. Learn to cultivate a balanced exchange, of energy inflow and release. Let empathy enter your spirit in the same way that the iris allows light into the retina. An iris operates within the fragility of the eyes—it adjusts it's diameter to focus and refract light beams, so that the brain accurately reports an experience. It is the same with vulnerability; make adjustments of emotion and empathy are minor and often, so that the full intention of a moment is felt. Open up to vulnerability, and life will open up to you.

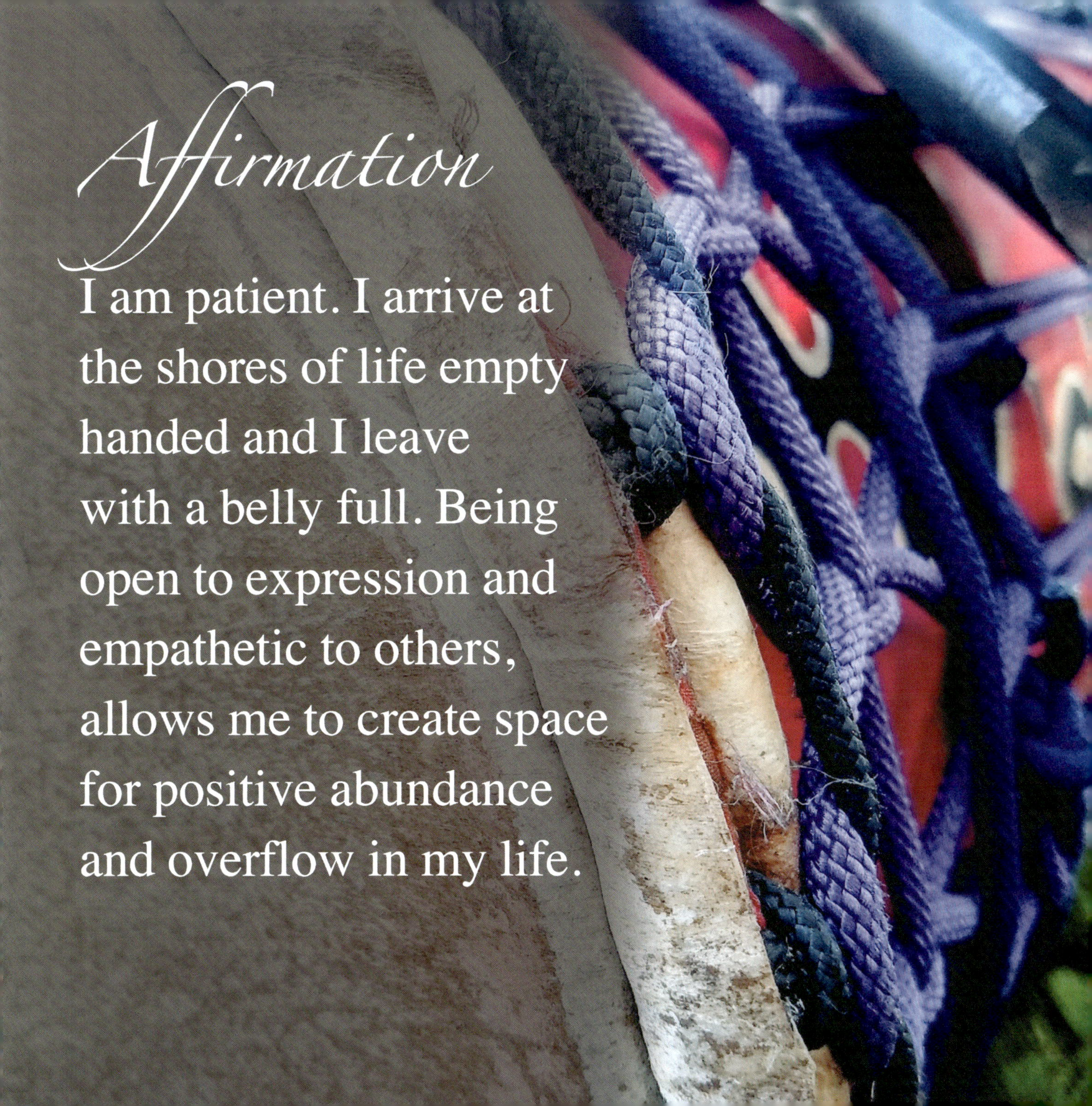

Affirmation

I am patient. I arrive at
the shores of life empty
handed and I leave
with a belly full. Being
open to expression and
empathetic to others,
allows me to create space
for positive abundance
and overflow in my life.

Mentoring 8

Mentoring takes place when a person with less knowledge, skill, or experience has ample time to observe, witness and rest in the presence of another with greater understanding. You can not mentor from a distance; mentoring requires presence. Use your personal values, principles, skill and knowledge and extend these traits to kids in the community who are not members of your household. A mentor does not see separation in community. If there are kids in the community, then they are your kids!

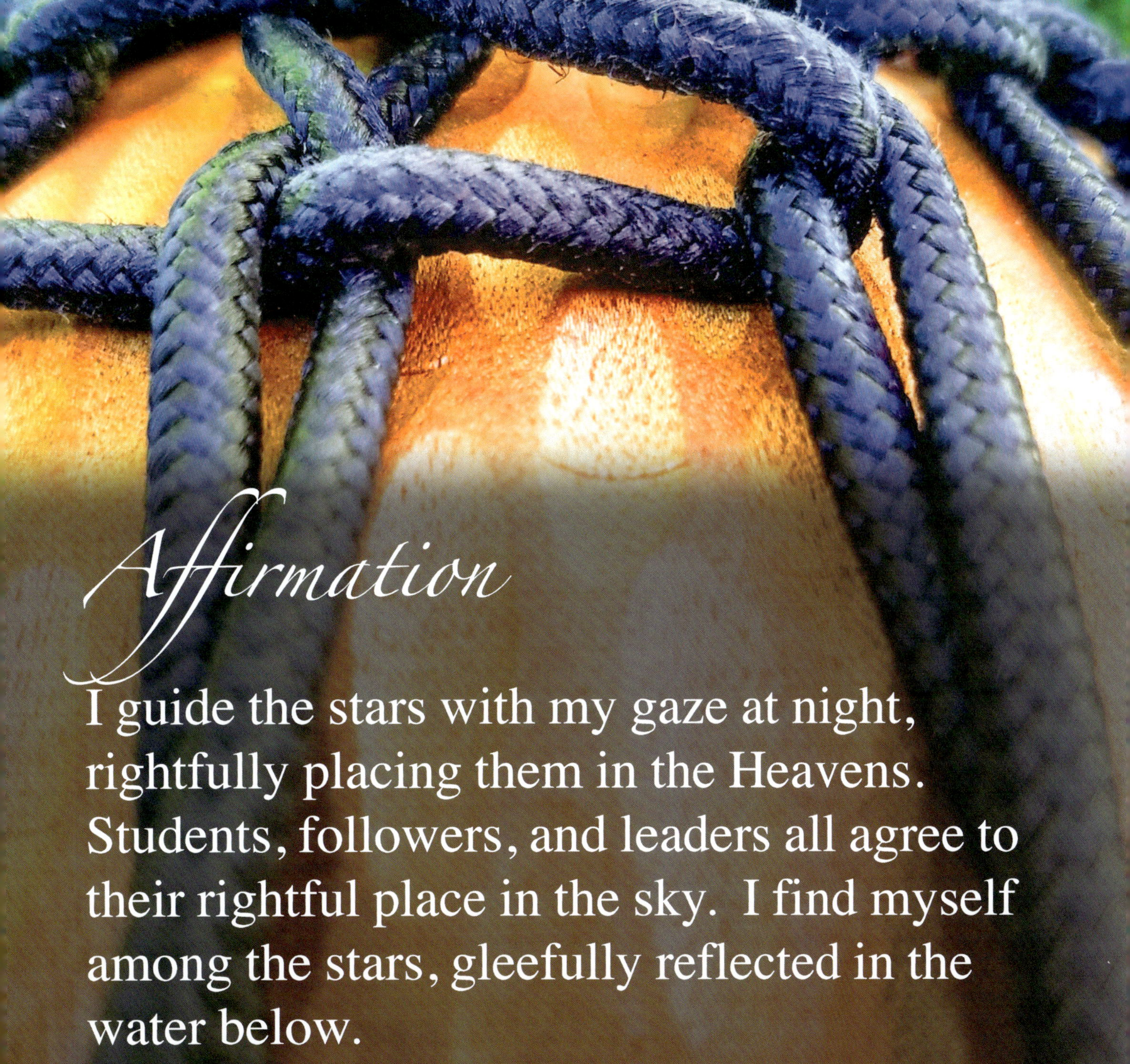

Affirmation

I guide the stars with my gaze at night,
rightfully placing them in the Heavens.
Students, followers, and leaders all agree to
their rightful place in the sky. I find myself
among the stars, gleefully reflected in the
water below.

Health 9

Wellness is absence of sickness and disease. It encompasses a comfortable life with little stress and distraction. Wellness contributes to health. However, without love and knowledge of self, and no understanding of self value, there can be no health. Sickness, insanity, depression and other ailments take root where love is not present. Learn first how to truly cultivate the value of loving yourself. Death arrives to us all someday; but healthy people greet death with a smiling heart.

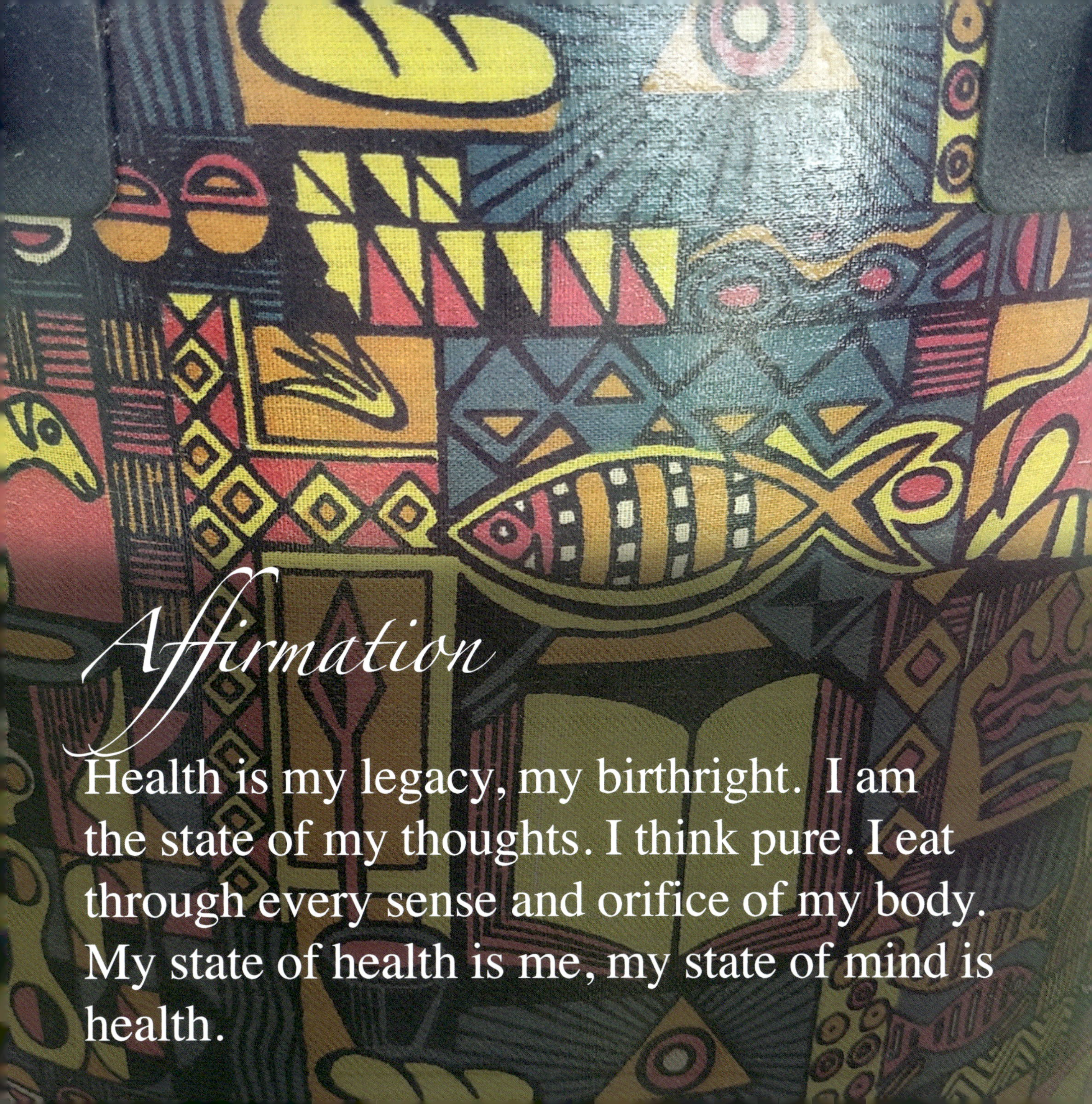

Affirmation

Health is my legacy, my birthright. I am the state of my thoughts. I think pure. I eat through every sense and orifice of my body. My state of health is me, my state of mind is health.

There are few things in
the world as dangerous
as sleepwalkers.
Ralph Ellison

Ritual 10

Order is peace, it is the manner in which the universe expresses itself, even chaos has a formula. Create and practice positive rituals in your life in order to cultivate energy that is conducive to bringing about harmony and eradicating all forms of dissonance. Yoga, prayer, and meditation, are all great forms of daily ritual — choose one, or choose many, but choose wisely, as improper habits lead to premature death.

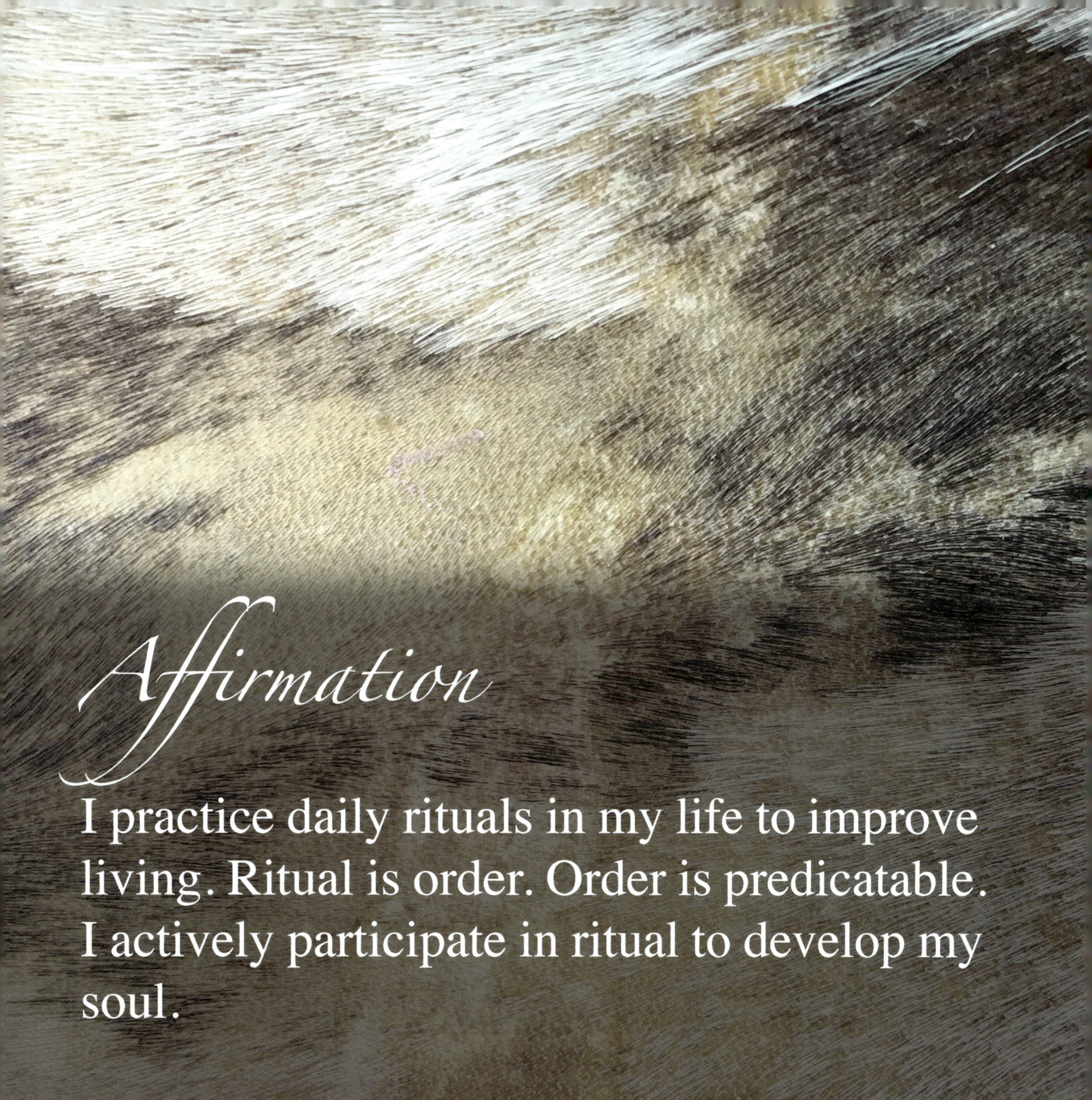

Affirmation

I practice daily rituals in my life to improve living. Ritual is order. Order is predicatable. I actively participate in ritual to develop my soul.

Empathetic Listening 11

Empathetic listening means listening with your full heart and attention. All connection happens through empathy. Especially when your children are very young and unable to express with words. Listen with your eyes, feel their cadence and tonality. Being listened to and attended to gives value to who your children are as people. Empathy is not sympathy nor judgment and doesn't happen while multi-tasking. Children want to inform, connect, and are expressing feeling to you as their parent. Expressing empathy is not sharing your testimony in the next breath after someone has finished speaking. Reflect what you hear or feel back to the person that shared. This doesn't mean you have to agree, but feeling heard is important for all human beings. The same may be said for friends, family and loved ones; we all want to feel heard and appreciated because then we know we are valued.

Affirmation

I listen with the full presence of my mind,
body, and awareness!

Anger 12

Anger has no place in the family. It is a caustic and destructive force. Anger expresses limitation and ego because the soul knows no capacity nor has it a boundary for love. "I am sorry," and "Please forgive me," are fertilizers for the soil of anger. These epithets are assurances that the tempest of anger will show itself once more when provoked. Many think that anger is natural. A primordial energy, anger was once used for slaughtering animals to eat or to defeat an enemy or foe. However, this obersvation is not true. Anger is a foreign substance, a viral agent to the soul. Spread it not in your household or community. Don't let it morph into a plague that develops different strains, such as mad, frustrated, pissed off, and upset. These strains of anger only seek to tear you down and your family apart. Instead, treat anger with preventative care. Keep a clean, healthy mind, purified thoughts and good intentions in the soul. This requires a daily ritual of introspective movement and thought to keep both the physical and astral bodies clean.

Affirmation

I am all that I see before me, between me, and around me. I am healthy of mind, body, and spirit. I control my will, my actions and my destiny.

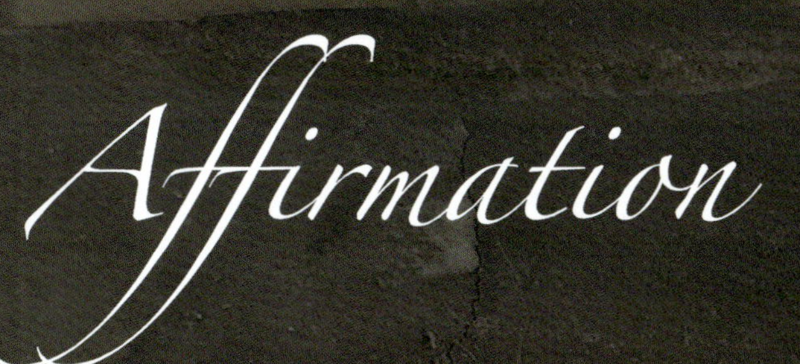

Forgiveness 13

Forgiveness is often the easiest thing to prescribe for someone else, yet the hardest pill to swallow for yourself. Forgiveness is a process. You can not simply wave your hand in the air in the sign of a cross, and suddenly all is forgiven. Once the need for forgiveness in a situation makes itself known, you will note that the action of forgiveness falls down like a set of dominoes: pain, frustration, and trauma run deep. An attempt to forgive one thing or person, often leads to a plethora of unresolved conflict within your mind for many other unjustifiable wrongs that have been committed against you. But the outcome of forgiveness begins and ends with releasing the ego and this overwhelming sense of "you-ness." Like a rip tide, one must surrender and lay limp in the cosmic energy of the push and pull process of forgiveness. Fear not that you will be lost in an ocean of rage. When the flow of forgiveness has released, swim diagonally across the tide, to a shore of mental stability and joy. The exercise of forgiveness itself will make you strong. Learn the art of surrender, acceptance, and letting-go. This is your first innerstanding of how to forgive.

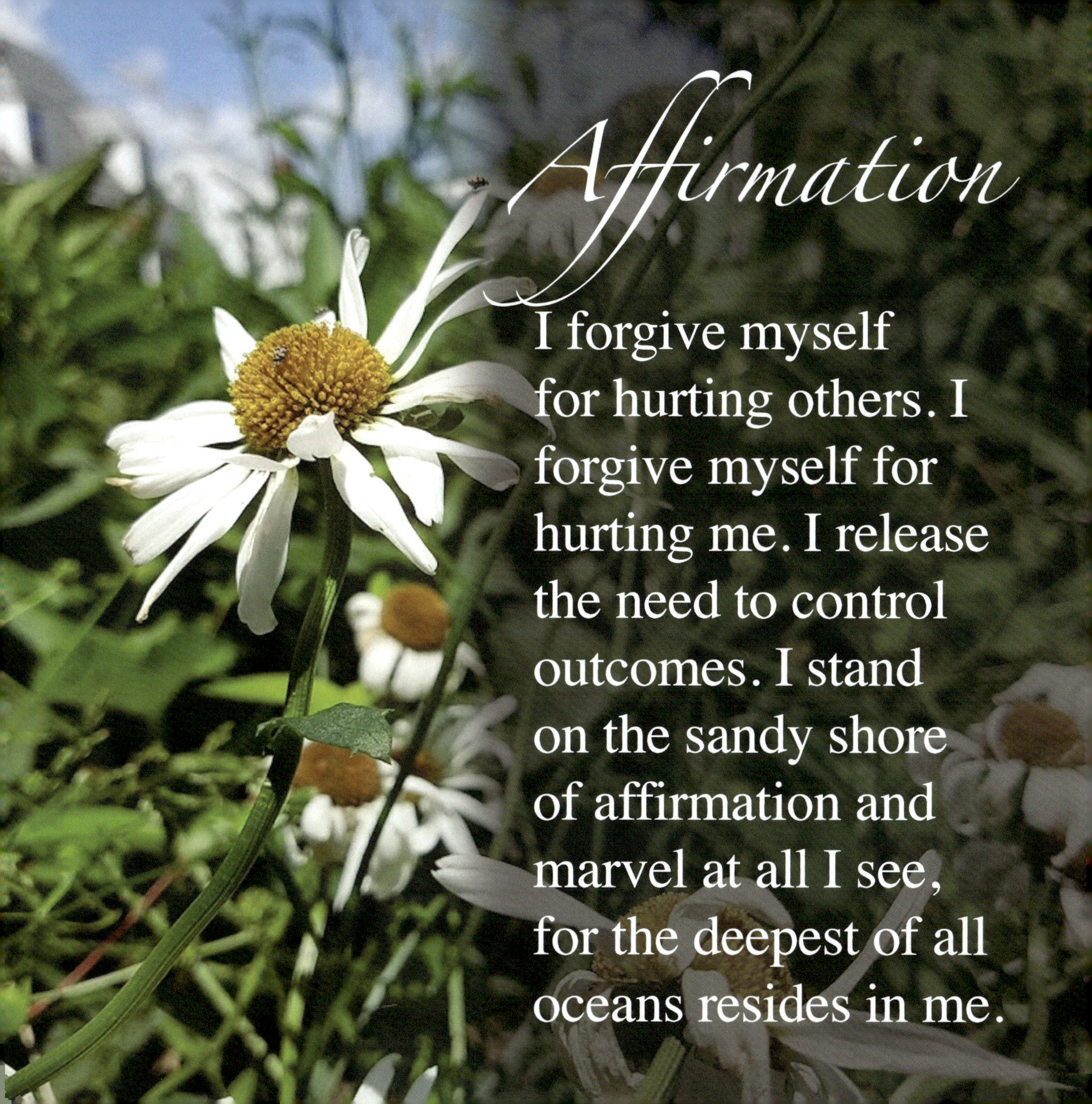

Affirmation

I forgive myself
for hurting others. I
forgive myself for
hurting me. I release
the need to control
outcomes. I stand
on the sandy shore
of affirmation and
marvel at all I see,
for the deepest of all
oceans resides in me.

Peaceful Warrior 14

I have learned to kill from lifetimes of living. Killing is neither wrong or right. I have killed time for no reason, plants and animals for which I eat, and I have killed other humans with my lying tongue. I have killed with deceit through both action and inaction. I have watched mighty and meek fall, but as a Peaceful Warrior I find unity in all. I bless all actions with spirit and love. I have defeated my own greed and replaced all things with love. As a Peaceful Warrior, I war not, rather I observe opposing forces curious of their maker. I have laid down my sword and weapon until being itself demands response. I am not the driver of the chariot, I am witnessing, I am unfolding, and I yield my will to discipline and obedience.

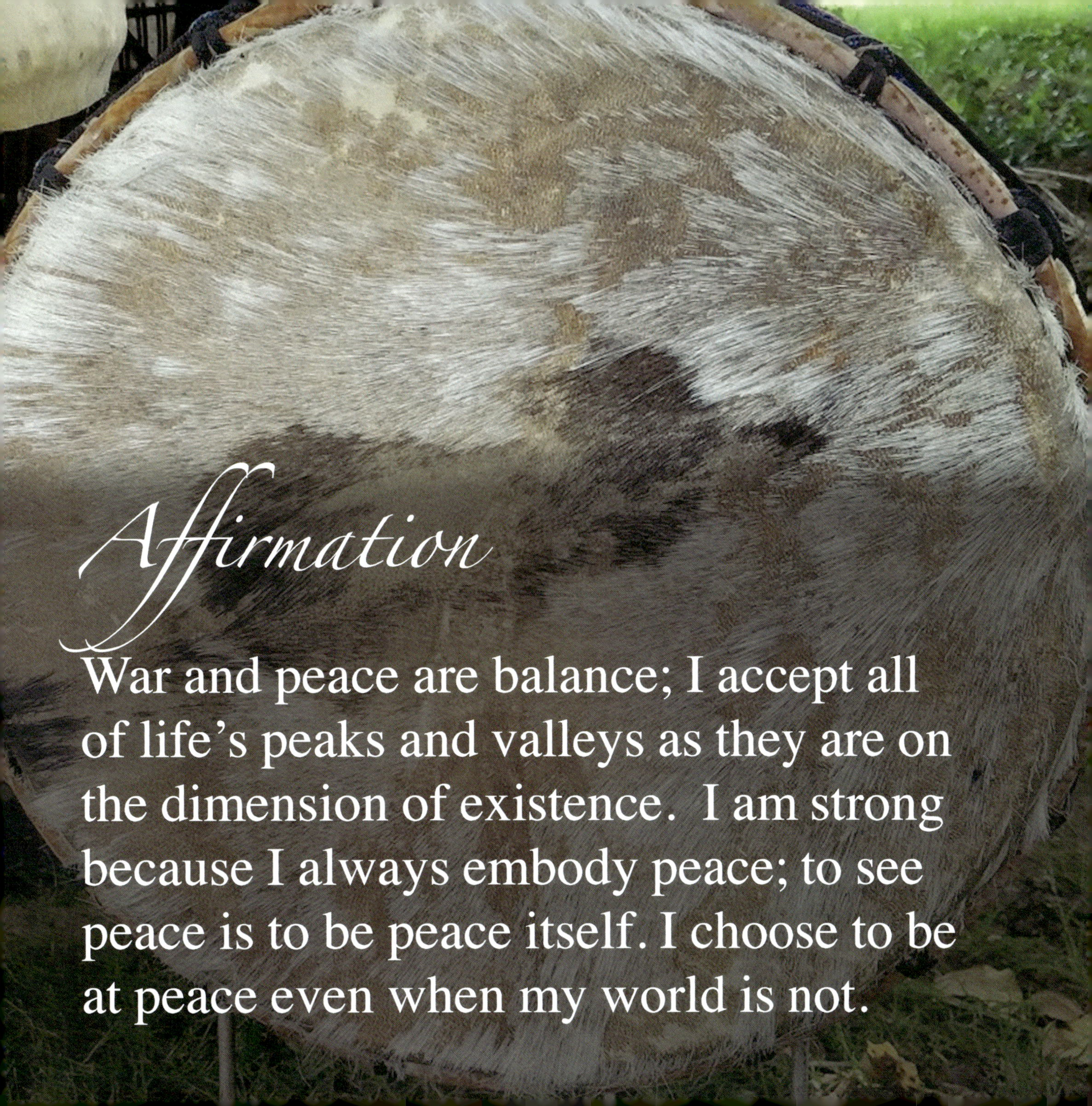
Affirmation
War and peace are balance; I accept all of life's peaks and valleys as they are on the dimension of existence. I am strong because I always embody peace; to see peace is to be peace itself. I choose to be at peace even when my world is not.

Cleansing & Fasting 15

Life itself is a ritual for cleansing the soul. If you truly understand this concept, the fear of death will leave you, and joy will fill your heart. Hygiene is not only cleanliness of the body, but of the emotional, intellectual and ephemeral bodies as well. Cleanse your mind with journaling or out-loud-conversations with nature, ancestors or self. Cry or laugh deeply to cleanse emotions. Sweat, practice deep-powerful breathing and eat whole foods like fruit and raw vegetables to cleanse the blood. Meditate or practice silence to cleanse the spirit. Do yoga or physical exercise to clean the body. All these things, we must do daily. Follow these methods, to cultivate a deserving temple for your soul.

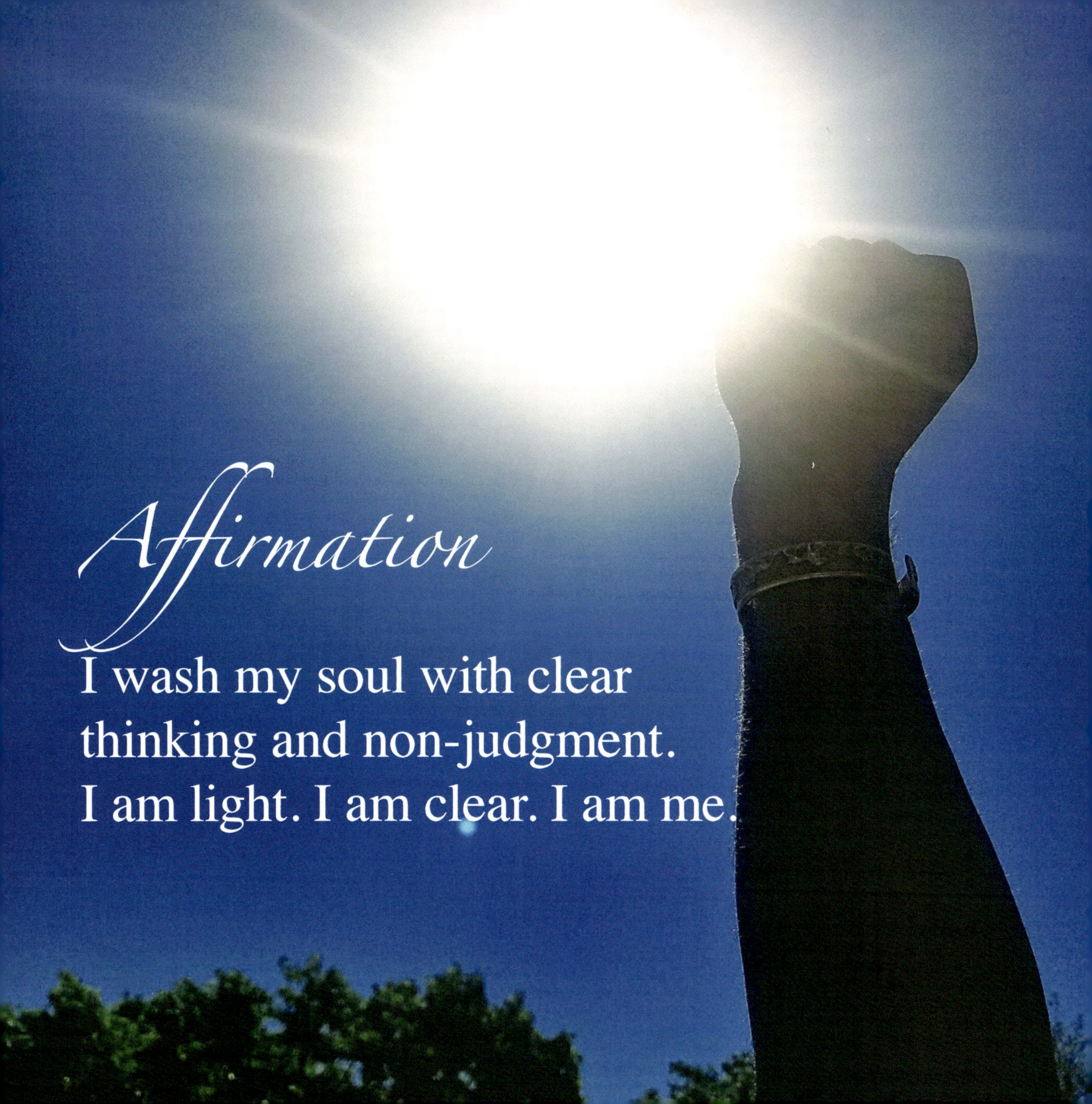

Affirmation

I wash my soul with clear
thinking and non-judgment.
I am light. I am clear. I am me.

Spiritual Warfare 16

As humans, we fear what we don't know. We use knowledge to fill the void within us created by terror and in an effort to remove our fears. What some label as voodoo, witchcraft, or devil-may-care, is yet unknown to them—the realm of the unknown is the cosmology of the Universe. In the vastness of the Universe, spiritual warfare takes place. Angels are energy, just as we are. Humans have been given the gift of consciousness and creation, along with the ability to harness war or peace within ourselves, and hence on the planet. Therefore, practice not spiritual warfare—do practice spiritual peace.

Affirmation

The spirit does not war with anyone
for all are spirit. I am equitable to all
man and womankind.

Sensory pleasure is a low-frequency modulation. Use the senses wisely. Don't let overly sweet become the norm. Pleasure is natural but not necessary. Cheating on a diet is the same as cheating on a spouse, because both involve integrity and a known truth about the best outcome, or at least the eventual outcome of the given circumstance. Yes, you may "have your cake and eat it too," just be sure you are clear on why you want both, and be ready to shoulder the outcome. All that appears to be in order, may not be ordained.

Affirmation

I lovingly accept all the Creator has given me. I have infinite gratitude for each opportunity life affords me.

Failure 18

Failure is a friend, period. Without it you would not be able to experience success. Accept failures when they happen. Be always ready for success. Victory may only be a failure away.

Affirmation

I see with accurate eyes and place no
judgment on life; as the sun rises, so do I.

One does not "find" time because we are an expression of time. If more time is needed one need look no further than one's self. If better time management is in order, then better self-management is needed. If more time to spend with family, kids, or a loved one is desired, don't "spend" time at all. Time is not currency, it is ever present. When we share time multitasking, or confounding presents with presence, we lose the proper perception of time. To be fully present in a moment of laughter, to hold a deep look in someone's eyes, or to hold hands so intimately that it produces an energetic exchange — this is what it means to be fully present in a moment. Intentionally being present, produces a feeling of oneness, not otherness — and it is that feeling of oneness that builds a reserve of time that lasts forever.

Affirmation

I have time. Time has me. We have each other, all is up to me.

20

There is no fixing or forgetting the past. The way to heal the past is through neutralization. Most of us do not know forgiveness. We know the definition of forgiveness and how to spell it, but if forgiveness were a person we wouldn't recognize them walking next to us down the street. What does the feeling of forgiveness feel like in the body? Where does it happen? Joy, is wrapped in forgiveness, the two are inseparable. Where you find forgiveness, you will find joy, and only then can the past be healed because it no longer exists. When joy has filled the heart, it washes away all pain and trauma of the past and reveals a rich, full, and vibrant expression of the present. In the fullness of the present moment, all gifts of life are identified and received.

Affirmation

I fill my heart with joy. I fill my soul with gladness. I have no room for empty spaces. My present moment is a timeless gift -- ripe with power, possibility and love.

Legacy 21

On the surface, legacy seems to be a tall order; it calls for abundance and strategy (at least in a Western context.) However, legacy at best, is short-lived and chaotic if it is not coupled with sustainability. Creating a sustainable world for all inhabitants: healthy air, water, earth and mind/body is the only legacy worth putting forth. Thinking and having forethought and concern at least 7 generations ahead, only scrapes the surface of what legacy can be. Yogis left us 3,000 years of legacy; Kemetians left us 5,000 years of legacy; this is love across gender, ethnicity and time. When we speak of legacy we do not speak at all—we do.

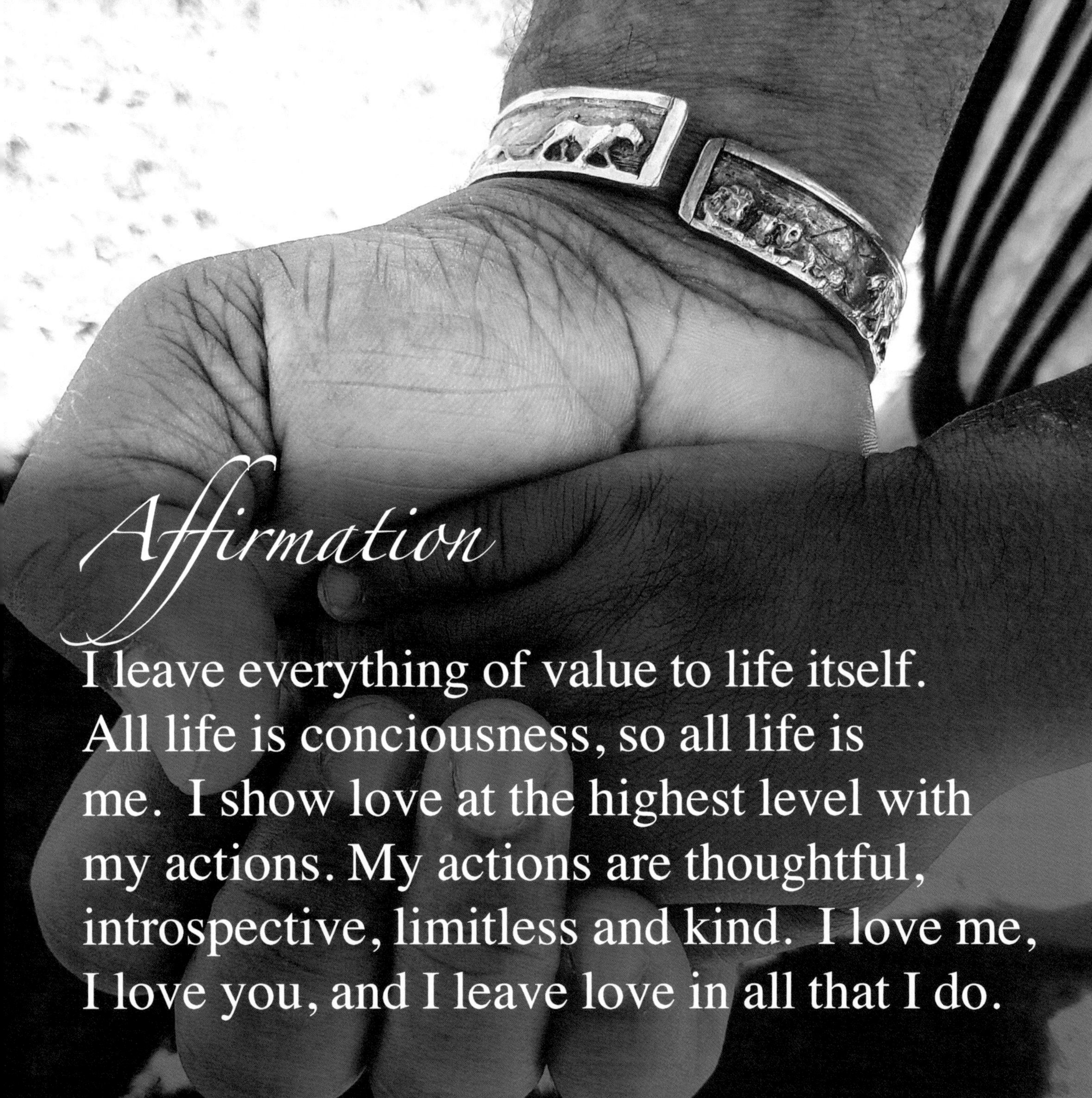

Affirmation
I leave everything of value to life itself.
All life is conciousness, so all life is
me. I show love at the highest level with
my actions. My actions are thoughtful,
introspective, limitless and kind. I love me,
I love you, and I leave love in all that I do.

He who cannot change
the very fabric of his thought,
will never be able to change
reality.
Anwar Sadat

Changa Bell is the founding Executive Director of The Black Male Yoga Initiative. Changa is a former film director and photographer who travelled, studied, and lived all over the world. He teaches the power of the narrative and the intricacies of mindfulness and how it relates to our daily lives. He is a purist who teaches Hatha yoga. Changa also is a health equity advocate and speaks around the world about the power of yoga, mindfulness, meditation and his LifeForce™ Development methodology. He lives in Baltimore, Maryland with his wife and 6 children.

Author photo by Glenwood Jackson

Visit Changa's website at
www.changabell.com

CPSIA information can be obtained at www.ICGtesting.com
Printed in the USA
BVIW12n0510050118
504499BV00001B/1